Aberdeenshire Library and Information Service
www.aberdeenshire.gov.uk/alis
Renewals Hotline 01224 661511

KENNEDY, Katharine

Housebreaking & other puppy
problems

Housebreaking & Other Puppy Problems

By Katharine Kennedy

INTRODUCTION

Who can deny the ever-growing popularity of dogs in our world? We can approximate that there are 250,000 puppies born each year that will need good owners and proper training. This book will help the new owner with the many problems to be faced as each puppy joins the family. It covers everything from the puppy's beginnings to housebreaking to what to do when the family's efforts aren't working. Best of all it features solutions to the many problems encountered while training a puppy—solutions that can be used today, tomorrow, and for years to come.

© by T.F.H. Publications, Inc.

Distributed in the UNITED STATES to the Pet Trade by T.F.H. Publications, Inc., One T.F.H. Plaza, Neptune City, NJ 07753; on the Internet at www.tfh.com; in CANADA Rolf C. Hagen Inc., 3225 Sartelon St. Laurent-Montreal Quebec H4R 1E8; Pet Trade by H & L Pet Supplies Inc., 27 Kingston Crescent, Kitchener, Ontario N2B 2T6; in ENGLAND by T.F.H. Publications, PO Box 15, Waterlooville PO7 6BQ; in AUSTRALIA AND THE SOUTH PACIFIC by T.F.H. (Australia), Pty. Ltd., Box 149, Brookvale 2100 N.S.W., Australia; in NEW ZEALAND by Brooklands Aquarium Ltd. 5 McGiven Drive, New Plymouth, RD1 New Zealand; in SOUTH AFRICA, Rolf C. Hagen S.A. (PTY.) LTD. P.O. Box 201199, Durban North 4016, South Africa; in Japan by T.F.H. Publications, Japan—Jiro Tsuda, 10-12-3 Ohjidai, Sakura, Chiba 285, Japan. Published by T.F.H. Publications, Inc.
MANUFACTURED IN THE
UNITED STATES OF AMERICA
BY T.F.H. PUBLICATIONS, INC.

CONTENTS

Photo Credits: Paulette Braun, Rhonda Dalton, Wil de Veer, Isabelle Francais, Chet Jezierski, Ermine Moreau-Sipere, Robert Pearcy, Sharron Podleski, Judith E. Strom, Karen Taylor.

Facing page: Puppies need lots of training and guidance to become well-mannered pets like Thornfield's Porsche Pride, owned by Christine Frank. He has earned his Utility Dog title in Obedience competition. Below: A posse of Old English Sheepdog puppies.

AMERICAN STAFFORDSHIRE TERRIER

Little Puppy, Big Responsibility

You are one of many millions who, each year, goes out and purchases a pet—in this instance a puppy. You did so, in all probability, without any working knowledge about the pet whose very life is going to depend totally on

Like these Rottweilers, all puppies are adorable when they are small. Without the proper training, however, they might grow to be unmanageable and destructive.

You must teach your children how to gently and carefully handle your new puppy.

that knowledge! Only as the weeks turn into months will you come to realize that things are not as simple as you had thought. That cute, cheeky little rascal that used to charge about your home with your slippers is now doing likewise with your best shoes. The little puddle on the carpet is now a sea of stains and smells, while that amusing high-pitched bark has become a monotonous howl that is driving your neighbors nuts!

If you purchased one of the larger breeds it is now growing up into a young adult. If you are not able to fully control the dog, things could become a real problem. The dog may become aggressive with strangers and be a positive danger near children. He may even turn that aggression on you and your family. By the time Fido has pigged the dinner you inadvertently left on the table while you answered the phone, and has rummaged a few times through the underwear in your washing basket, you just might begin to wonder whether owning a puppy was the most sensible thing you have done.

Maybe you have seen

Being a responsible dog owner means teaching your puppy to respect and behave properly with all members of your family.

A puppy may be easier to train than an adult dog, but no dog is untrainable. Practice, persistence and patience pay off!

the amber warning light, which is why you purchased this book, or maybe (ideally) you have not actually obtained your puppy and want to learn how to train it before problems become *fait accompli*. Whatever the reasons, you have taken a very positive step. You clearly want to become a responsible owner. No dog is untrainable, though some are most certainly easier than others. Further, if you are starting with a puppy you will have less problems than if you acquired an adult—unless the latter has already been trained.

Your puppy won't know you don't want him in or on certain things unless you teach him what's off-limits. These repellents can quicken the lesson. They can be used indoors and out, and they're completely safe. Courtesy of Four Paws.

DALMATIAN

Your Puppy's Very Beginnings

The personality of a puppy is determined by the collective effect of a number of factors. It is important that you recognize these because they will to a very large degree influence just how easy, or difficult, it will be to train your pet.

1. Genes: Each puppy is born with a given potential not only in respect of its size, color, and other conformation features, but also with regards to traits.

These include intelligence, docility, aggression, resistance to disease, breeding vigor, motherhood, and other less easily monitored characteristics. Some dogs have an inborn predisposition towards certain traits, and we recognize these in the form of guarding, herding, retrieving, hunting, and fighting breeds. Other breeds, and cross-bred dogs, have no obvious inclinations to perform a specific function, thus

show no given trait to a noticeable degree. They are very adaptable.

2. The Environment: To what degree the genetic potential of a puppy is achieved will be totally dependent on the environment in which it is raised. The environment includes a number of areas—nutrition, housing, general attention to health, and the way in which the puppy is socialized, or not, with people, other dogs,

A dog's personality is shaped by the different experiences and influences he encounters from birth. It is up to you, the owner, to bring up your puppy in the most positive atmosphere possible.

Your puppy's mother has a great influence on the health and personality of your pet. A happy and healthy mother has a better chance of producing happy and healthy puppies.

barker, or is nervous, or frightened, this is transposed to her puppies. The senses develop rapidly. By the time it is about three weeks old, a puppy is becoming very aware of the world in which it lives, and in which it is now moving around. If it is being reared in substandard conditions where it is forced to attend its toilet needs where it sleeps, it will prove to be a much more difficult puppy to housebreak. If its mother is subjected to abuse, this will be impregnated in its tiny mind and it will always be a more difficult dog to truly socialize as it grows up. It may become a very fearful puppy. If it is roughly handled by its breeder this will have a totally negative effect on

other animals, and a range of environmental situations (for example, busy streets, motor cars, domestic appliances, and so on).

3. The Puppy's Mother: Your puppy's mother clearly has a tremendous influence on the personality of her offspring. This influence commences even before the puppy is born! Her own physical condition at the time she becomes pregnant will determine many aspects of her offspring's physical state. As the embryo develops it is continually influenced by the state of the female at any given time.

Once a pup is born it may not be able to see or even hear but it is able to

sense what is going on around it. If its mother is a

Just like us, puppies are what they eat and are affected by their diet. One that combines the natural nutrients of quality meats and vegetables can provide a growing puppy with all he needs. Photo courtesy of Nature's Recipe Pet Foods.

Your puppy's relationship with his littermates is an important one. He will learn how to interact with other dogs by playing and living with his siblings when he is young.

its future attitude to humans. If it is subjected to abuse by other older puppies or dogs, this will affect its view of its own kind. Much, therefore, happens from the time a puppy is born until the time it arrives in your home.

The more stable its early life, the more reliable its personality will be as it grows up. If a puppy is taken from its mother and siblings at too early an age, this may have two effects. It may more easily become bonded with humans but, depending on events in the following weeks, it may develop very negative personality traits, such as nervousness, aggression, or shyness. The believed benefits of imprinting pets with humans early in their lives is now being challenged. It would seem that a crucial aspect is not just removing the puppy from its mother but the fact that it is removed from its siblings,

with whom it learns how to interact and take the rough and tumbles of life.

PUPPY SOURCES

From this you can appreciate that weeks three to eight are cornerstones in shaping the personality of a puppy. All else that follows will be influenced by what has happened during that critical period, as well as what subsequently happens. The source of a puppy will obviously be a most important factor in shaping the character of the puppy, for better or for worse. It is therefore perti-

nent to our discussion to consider the various sources from which you may have purchased your pup, or from where you may be thinking of buying it. You may not have thought about the points raised here, so they may save you from making a costly mistake.

If, however, you have already obtained your puppy, its source might explain certain problems with which you are already confronted, or that may start to display themselves in the not-too-distant future.

If your puppy gets a good start in life, he will become a loving and devoted companion.

GERMAN SHEPHERD DOG

A Wolf in Puppy's Clothing

In order to more fully appreciate your puppy, what he thinks and what he does not, you must detach your mind from the tendency to apply anthropomorphic qualities to him. If you understand how the puppy would lead his life in the wild, you can be more sympathetic to those features of his character that you may find personally disagreeable. You will also appreciate why dogs are called "man's best friend" and why they can, given correct training, fit so perfectly into a family unit. And you will appreciate just how and why dogs can become delinquent in human society.

There is now little disagreement in zoological circles that the dog is the domesticated form of the gray wolf, *Canis lupus.* This wolf is a highly gregarious animal for the most part, but is quite able to live a solitary life if conditions dictate. The pack is the basic social unit, made up of a male, female, and their offspring of one or more years. The pairing of the male and female is invariably for life, indicating the very strong bonding that these animals have. The family unit will normally comprise about five to eight individuals, but packs of up to thirty-six have been recorded.

CANID SOCIAL STRUCTURE

The social structure within the wolf pack is hierarchal and often based on a superior (alpha) male and his chosen female, though a female may be the leader in some packs. The hierarchy is not a simple line of dominance based on muscle power, though this is how the alpha leader attains power. There is clear evidence that both the pack leader and his mate head their own hierarchal structures. Favoritism plays a part in the social life of wolves as much as it does in human society, so it can be a case of not what you are but who you know!

The wolf pack will live within a given territory, which may be small or large depending on the availability of prey species.

It is not a good idea to apply human qualities to your dog – dogs do not think like people. The more you understand how your puppy thinks, the better your relationship will be with him.

Unlike their wolf ancestors, our dogs depend on us to provide them with adequate diets—especially growing pups, pregnant or lactating females, and very active or working dogs. Choose the best you can. Photo courtesy of Nature's Recipe Pet Foods.

The territory is aggressively defended against would-be intruders; as a result, wolf pack territories tend to rarely overlap. Instead, there is generally a "no-go" buffer area between each pack's territory.

When a female wolf has her litter, the cubs are fed by the pack as a whole, as is the female, who remains near the den to attend her offspring. As the cubs grow up they are taken on hunts and taught how to track and attack their prey, which is invariably larger than they are. The survival of the pack is totally dependent on the cooperation between its members. Each has a place in the hierarchy and will only move up if it gains

great strength or has much determination—or with the passage of time and the weakness of older members. Alternatively, it may leave the pack and seek a a lone member of the opposite sex from another pack. This process ensures future genetic heterozygosity within the family lines.

HOW STATUS CHANGES

Given the system by which a pack operates, which is actually much the same as with we humans, it follows that all members are subservient to a single leader. Were this not the case the entire social structure of the wolf pack would collapse. Any

Each dog has his place in the hierarchy of the pack, and the pack is dependent on each member's cooperation for survival. This Australian Cattle Dog mom tends to the needs of her pup, just like the wolf mother takes care of her cubs.

individual that ventures to either move up the hierarchal ladder or challenge for the leadership does so at no small risk to its health. When such challenges are made the challenger may win, or may be severely hurt in the process. He or she may even be chased from the pack and forced to become a lone wolf until he or she can strike up an association with another loner, or maybe join another small unit that is in the process of forming. Once again, the new member must sort out its position in the new structure.

When a new leader eventually takes over a pack it can have a dramatic effect on the way the social ladder is arranged. It is a period of considerable tension and disharmony for the entire pack. As a result, there is a sort of inbuilt safety mechanism that maintains the stability of the pack for as long as is possible. If the leader is despotic, his or her leadership will vanish the minute the ability to rule wholly by force becomes challengeable. But if the leader shows wisdom and fairness in the way he or she rules, their chances of surviving as a leader may well exceed their actual power to enforce that leadership. In other words, a wolf can assert authority by its forbearance and general demeanor without the need to be forever proving that it is the strongest and most aggressive member of the pack. It gains respect out of its leadership qualities, and the rest of the pack is happy to recognize and accept that leadership.

Pups learn the rules of pack order through interacting with their littermates. However, once a puppy becomes part of a human family "pack," the owner assumes the role of pack leader and must not let the pup assert his dominance.

All dogs communicate with each other through body language, a skill picked up from adults when they are puppies. This German Shorthaired Pointer looks like he is ready to play!

COMMUNICATION

Wolves communicate with each other, and with other packs, by any of four basic means: facial expressions, body language, vocalizations, and scent. Facial expressions include the baring of fangs by lip movements, and eye contact. Body postures include the lowering of the ears, raising or lowering the tail, raising of the fur on the neck, the moving of the head to one side, lowering the head, rolling on their backs, and crawling forwards on their belly. Through these various postures they are able to indicate submissiveness or defiance.

By adopting a submissive posture, such as crawling, lowering the tail, rolling over and baring the teeth in a very characteristic manner, they are able to avoid what otherwise might result in fights and injury. When fights do occur they will end when the loser takes a submissive stance, while the victor will stand over the loser for a given short span of time. The matter is then over and status is confirmed.

Status is determined when the wolf is a cub. When playing with other cubs it will go through all of the motions that it has seen the adults doing. In this way, by the time it is old enough to inflict serious injury, its standing in relation to its siblings is established, so there is no need to fight these. A strong-willed youngster, with the possible help of aunts and uncles or parents, will move up through the ranks and achieve a given adult status. A weaker pup will always be a low-ranking individual. This it will accept without problem. Likewise, the higher-ranked members will not pick on it unless it transgresses some wolf code, when it will be attacked and shown just why it is low in rank. As a low member it will have to wait for the higher members to eat before it can get food, and the chances of passing on its genes are slim. In this way, only the genes of high ranking members will be passed on to form the next generation.

Vocalizations are in the form of growling, whining, whimpering and, of course, howling. It was often thought that howling was a sound of exuberance by the pack members, but it is now believed that it is basically a call of communication. It lets other pack members know

Status in the pack is determined when wolves are cubs, and puppies, like their wolf ancestors, develop either dominant or submissive personalities through interaction with their littermates.

where each other is, and it also tells other packs where territorial boundaries are. Each wolf has its own distinctive howl.

Scent marking is very important to wolves. The scent is urine, which is deposited at given intervals on trees, rocks, shrubs or whatever. It tells members of other packs where boundaries are. It also tells the males the sexual state of a female. Again, the members of a pack each have their own

HUNTING

When wolves hunt they test many individuals to see which display a weakness. They do this by running alongside the prey to prompt them to run. Most hunts are failures, so the pack must be resilient and be prepared to test many times before they find a suitable prey. This will normally be a young, old, or injured animal. The main prey will be caribou, moose, deer, musk ox or beaver when times are

cubs. They will devote much time to playing with the babies. This is an essential part of the bonding that is so vital to a species that relies heavily on the cooperative efforts of all members in order to survive. As the youngsters grow up, so they are taught not only what their status is in the pack, but what is and is not acceptable.

Within the social organization of wolves you can see just why dogs—more so than any other animal—fit in so well with humans.The lifestyle of the wolf mirrors that of humans to an uncanny level. It is complex, and for success depends on a very close interaction between the individuals. When a puppy or dog enters your household it does not become humanized but, rather, in its eyes you simply become the pack. As such it will defend territory (your home) and the other pack members (your family, which may extend to other pets). The dog has an built-in need to be part of a society. As such, it accepts authority without question. If such leadership is not forthcoming it has no option but to become the leader itself.

A strong-willed dog will accept leadership, but it may constantly test it if it is perceived to be weak. You cannot have a situation with a dog where

Hunting for food is an instinct in all members of the canine family, starting from when they are "cubs" and continuing through adulthood.

scent and this is known to all of the pack. They are able to discern how old a scent is, thus how far away another wolf may be. Floor scratching, fecal matter, and regular urination are also forms of scent marking.

hard. But they will also take birds, rats, mice, snakes and carrion if big game is not plentiful.

CUB REARING

All members of the pack share in the duty of raising and training the

Your gentle and sweet puppies may look far removed from their wild ancestors, but they share a lot of the same qualities, a fact which is helpful to remember when training your dog.

you are *almost* in charge, because this is intolerable to the dog. It will slowly grind away at that *almost* until it becomes "sort of," and eventually the dog rules the house.

Within your family every member must establish a status in relation to the dog. Your pet must be subservient to all, otherwise problems will arise. However, in saying subservient this does not suggest that status should be gained by brute force, for as you have seen superiority based on such is tenuous and unreliable.

Like a wolf, a dog is quick to recognize it can gain status by favoring a given family member, to whom it will turn to get privileges and/or special protection. It does not reason this out (as far as we can tell) but instinctively knows which members of the human pack can best serve its own interests.

Your dog may no longer possess the same level of natural cunning or acute senses of its wild ancestors, but beneath that veneer of docility and domestication there still lies a wild animal that

thinks and acts just as the wolf does. Your objective is to try and modify its behavior patterns such that they enable your pet to function as an integral member of its adopted pack. This means it must be treated as a pack member and not as though it were some cuddly, mindless entity that you expect to think and act as though it was human. If you can do this the rewards of loyalty, affection, and willingness to please will be yours for its entire life.

If you treat your puppy with respect and affection and clearly convey to him your expectations about his behavior, you will be rewarded with a loyal and loving companion for life.

BORDER COLLIE

Do You Have What it Takes to Train a Dog?

Any trainer who is involved with owners and their dogs will tell you the greater part of the lessons is not so much training the dogs as the owners. Too often owners compare dogs with human children, assuming that if they've brought up children it should be easy to bring up a dog. There are some valid comparisons but, in general, if you have never trained a dog before (or failed in previous attempts) you should commence by

Above: Puppies are full of boundless energy. You will need a lot of patience and stamina to stay consistent with a training regimen. Below: The puppy is not the only pupil in the training process. The owner must learn the proper training methods as well, in order to get the optimum performance from his dog. This is Mc. Williams Never Offside, owned by Wil de Veer.

emptying your mind of any preconceived notions on the subject.

Here's a quick and easy quiz to help you gauge your own strengths and weaknesses relating to your ability to train your puppy. Answer them honestly (or let your wife, husband or another family member answer them for you!).

1. Are you short tempered?

2. Do you quickly get frustrated if things do not go as well as you had hoped?

3. Are you inconsistent in the way you judge people?

Puppies do not learn through intimidation or violence; rather, they respond best to consistent training and praise when they do well. If you wish to train your puppy yourself, you must develop trust between you and your dog.

4. Do you give up on hobbies easily in order to try new ones?

5. Once you begin a training session do you believe it should be completed come what may?

6. If your dog had committed a misdemeanor and you called it to you, would you spank it for this, say "No" in a firm voice, or praise the dog?

7. Are you a very retiring, placid sort of person?

8. Do you enjoy walking and generally being out and about?

9. Do you nag your marital partner or your children?

10. Are you a show-off?

Let us review the questions and see how your response might affect your ability as a trainer.

1. If you admit to being short-tempered this is a black mark against you and something you will definitely have to work on. You cannot afford to display inadequacies when training. You will frighten and frustrate your puppy and make training totally impossible.

2. If you get frustrated easily this is another black mark because I assure you that when training a puppy you will at times be at your wit's end to understand why a given command is not being understood, or why your puppy persists in a given action. This is when a calm and reasoning mind is needed.

3. If you are inconsistent in your judgment of people you will probably be likewise with your puppy. This is not at all good. Inconsistency can reinforce unwanted behavior patterns as well as create new ones.

4. If you give up on things easily the chances are you will give up on your puppy the minute you reach a stumbling block. You will find excuses why you cannot take your dog for a walk, why you have skipped the last few training sessions, and will no doubt find reasons why your puppy is not doing well—and not one of the reasons will include yourself.

5. The answer is, it should not. If you think it should, this suggests you are too much of a disciplinarian or too rigid in your attitude. Lessons should only be completed if both you and the dog are making satisfactory progress and are clearly in the mood for the lesson.

6. This question tests your notions about training. The answer is praise the dog—you will understand why as you read the book.

If you want to tackle training your dog yourself, you must be willing to get outside and do some hands-on exercises with your puppy.

7. If you answered yes to this, fine. But you must take care that you do not let your mild nature result in your puppy becoming the master. You might have problems with any of the strong-willed dogs, so be careful what you choose.

8. I hope so, because you will need to get out and about quite a lot with your puppy in order to both train and socialize him to the human world. A puppy that does not get out and meet people may develop aggression, fear, or other undesirable hang-ups created by excessive confinement.

9. If you are a nagger you must work on curbing this where your puppy is concerned or it will fail to understand commands and become frustrated, which in turn will prompt you to nag more, thus compounding an already undesirable situation.

10. It's one thing to show off your car, your home, or other material possessions, but it can be a problem to show off a puppy you are training. Prematurely demonstrating how well the training is going could backfire if the pup is not totally sure of its commands. This will erode both yours and the puppy's confidence.

IF YOU PASSED

A good trainer should be possessed of unlimited patience and compassion, yet have the ability to be

Proper obedience training is a responsibility you owe to your dog. You will find the time you spend in training to be a rewarding and fulfilling experience.

firm when this is needed. A trainer must have an inquiring mind in order that problems can be analyzed and logical solutions devised. The trainer must then have the conviction to follow through on a course of action if this is believed to be the one most appropriate to the situation. A trainer must always be prepared to accept new techniques and ideas, but not just because they are fashionable. New concepts must be well considered so that their weaknesses are balanced against any merits they may obviously display.

Trainers must have enthusiasm for the task and for what they believe in. They must be consistent in their actions, and at all times be in full control of their emotions.

After all, if you cannot control your own temper or emotions, you can hardly expect your dog to control its internal desires and instincts—yet this is what you are expecting it to do.

IF YOU FAILED

I believe it is better to train your own dog than to have a professional do it for you. This is because you will build a stronger bond with your dog and have greater pride in its achievements. This said, if you are honest enough to concede that you flunked on the above questionnaire, you would be doing yourself and your puppy a favor by letting a professional trainer effect the pup's education.

If you think carefully about the points raised in this chapter you will see that even if you may not

think you are a suitable trainer at this moment, the reality is that you can become so if you are determined enough to make the needed effort. You can enroll in an obedience class to work with a professional, or hire someone to work with the dog one-on-one. Group classes are great for socializing your puppy while you work with him. But to be totally honest, I would suggest that if you really flunked the questions a dog may not be the most satisfactory pet for you. In the final analysis it comes down to the question of whether or not you love your puppy enough to want to make sure it can live a wholesome life of security within your family. The fact that you are reading this book would suggest that you do.

Taking your pup to obedience class is an option if you feel you may need guidance or assistance in training your pet. You can get professional help and let your dog socialize with other puppies at the same time.

Providing your pup with the proper training shows that you care about his well-being and his future as a member of your family.

PUG

ASSESSING YOUR PUPPY'S PERSONALITY

The factors that influence the personality of a dog are the conditions it is living under, its past treatment, the way it is exposed to many situations, and most of all by the way its owner has tackled the job of training it. These aspects are changing steadily as the puppy grows up, and every puppy is different. Getting a sense of how your puppy responds to things will, however, greatly aid your training. Is your puppy naturally reserved; dominant; secure; excessively

Some puppies have very active personalities and others are much more mellow. You must choose your dog by deciding which type of personality best fits your lifestyle.

Every dog is an individual – some are reserved, some dominant, some inherently curious. Do not prejudge your dog's personality before observing him closely in different situations.

nervous? With careful observation you will be able to assess your puppy's personality, thereby assisting both your training and your relationship.

PERSONALITY BY OBSERVATION

The advantage of judging personality by observation is that you are not so readily tempted to label your puppy and draw assertive conclusions one way or the other, then base your training program on such conclusions. It allows you to monitor many more reactions, and in a natural rather than forced manner.

As with any worthwhile study, you should make notes of your observations. Jot them on a notebook you carry with you whenever you are with the puppy, or speak into a pocket tape recorder. If you do not take this approach you may overlook some seemingly unimportant happening. This may later be a clue that could help you to unravel a problem the pup develops.

WHAT YOU SHOULD OBSERVE

Observation begins the moment you get your puppy. The following is a list of numerous situations, people, objects, and sounds to which you will note the puppy's reaction. You can expand on this one to compile your own list, which can be as lengthy as you are prepared to make it.

If you consider carefully the numerous questions, you will find that they will not only tell you something about your puppy's personality but also pinpoint aspects of its behavior patterns that may need immediate attention. This way you can stop the behavior before it is reinforced. Collectively, the questions may give some indication of how the puppy has been previously treated. After each question a few guiding comments are given.

1. Was the puppy upset or relaxed when being transported home? Was it sick?

Comment: This will not tell you much about the pup's personality, but it will obviously tell you whether it may experience upsets in the future when traveling in a vehicle. However, you need to know how long before the trip home the puppy was fed. Clearly, the momentum of the trip will more readily upset a full stomach.

2. When given the opportunity to explore its new home did the puppy do so confidently with its tail held high, or was it very apprehensive and carrying its tail low? If it showed variable reaction note which rooms or objects seemed to concern it.

Comment: The well-balanced puppy will explore in a confident manner, tail held high, ears erect, but will show momentary caution when it sees an object it is unfamiliar with. If it is a bold dog it will probably growl and bark at such objects, moving around them to search for a vulnerable spot (as would a wild dog). The dog that shows great caution and keeps its tail low may be a nervous or very shy dog, or one that has never seen the inside of a home so is very wary of all that it sees. You will get a better idea of its emotional state by observing its reactions outdoors and comparing them.

3. When first meeting other family members or friends, did your puppy go to them willingly, wagging its tail; go to them but crawl submissively when it reached them; or run and hide?

Comment: The well-socialized puppy will have no problems approaching strangers. It will keep its tail high and wagging. The speed with which it approaches strangers will indicate just how confident it is in itself. If it moves submissively to other people this suggests that it has either received rough treatment at the hands of humans or other dogs. If it also urinates you can assume it has been

One of the many ways you can assess your puppy's personality is by watching his reaction to traveling in a car. If he seems easily upset or sick, he may be overly nervous.

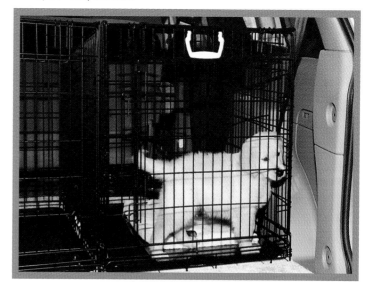

physically disciplined far too often for its young age. If it runs away it has a problem, because it is clearly very frightened of people, which can only mean these have given it cause to be, or has led an extremely isolated life.

4. How did it react to other pets in the home, if any? Did it run from them, go to them, chase them, or stand and bark at them?

Comment: A puppy that chases, goes to, or stands and barks, is displaying a normal healthy attitude. This does not mean chasing or barking are desirable in the human pack the puppy is to live with. Fleeing from other small pets would indicate a bad previous experience

The well-socialized puppy will be willing to explore and will be confident when faced with new surroundings or new people. This Dalmatian looks ready to take on the world!

where the puppy was bitten, scratched, or chased by other animals, including dogs.

5. When you pick the puppy up does it seem apprehensive or very happy to be near you?

The way a puppy behaves with his littermates tells a lot about his personality; it's easy to pick out which pups are shy and which are more dominant.

Comment: The confident, well-adjusted puppy will wish to shower you with affection. It will have no inhibitions at all about this. If it seems apprehensive, this would indicate it is either very shy and timid by nature, has had little previous socialization with humans, or is not sure what to expect, meaning it may have received a few smacks in the past. It may also have been dropped or roughly handled on more than one occasion, maybe by a child.

6. When it hears a noise,

These Shiba Inu and Boxer puppies have no problem getting along with each other. Early socialization is the key to ensuring that your dog will be friendly and well-behaved when exposed to other animals.

such as the door banging, the vacuum cleaner, a can being dropped, or any other sudden sound, does it flee under a chair; appear startled initially but not run away; or appear startled and then approach the source of the noise?

Comment: Any pup should be startled by a sudden noise, just as you would be. If it is a bold pup with an outgoing nature it will seek out the source, albeit cautiously. If it flees this would indicate a rather nervous individual that is either inherently timid or has been badly frighted by noises in the past.

7. When you are stroking it does it seem unconcerned where you touch it, or does it show some reluctance to let you touch a given part of its body?

Comment: A normal reaction is to be unconcerned, the only reaction being for the pup to want to bite on your hand in a playful manner.

A well-behaved, well-socialized puppy should be very willing to have you pet him and should quickly become accustomed to being groomed.

It is hard to resist giving this cuddly Chow Chow puppy, Ch. Rebelrun's Starlite Knight, a squeeze. Your puppy should revel in the affection you give him.

A well-adjusted puppy will be active and playful with people and other dogs. This eight-week-old Bernese Mountain Dog romps enthusiastically with his mother.

A reluctance to be touched on certain parts of the body would indicate either a tender spot from a recent injury, a current health problem, inherent timidity, or the fact that someone has previously hurt the puppy at that bodily point.

8. Does it display any fear reaction if you bend over in front of it in order to stroke it, or does it simply jump straight up at you for fuss?

Comment: It should launch itself at you with vigor. If it is of a rather submissive nature it may not hurl itself with quite the same gusto, or may even roll over at your feet. If it rolls over, urinates, or cringes it has been physically struck by its previous owner on more than one occasion.

9. Does it whine and bark when left alone for short periods, or at night when you go to bed (assuming the puppy is not sleeping on the bed)?

Comment: If it is quiet then this indicates it has

become used to being left alone. It has been separated from its siblings for long enough not to be missing them. If it cries this is a normal reaction for a puppy recently separated from its mother, its siblings, or a breeder who kept it with them when they retired for the night.

10. When taken out for a walk note how it reacts to a range of stimuli. These include other dogs, cats, birds, cars, people and their situations. The latter means are there a lot of people about, or few.

Comment: From these observations you can get an insight into both its inherent nature and its previous exposure status to the world around it. A normal puppy will be very curious about wildlife and will wish to chase, or least

explore the point where it was seen. It will stand boldly and stare, with ears erect, and may bark at strange things. If it shows anxiety and overt fear then it has never been exposed to the outside world, and is of a rather timid nature. Alternatively, it may have received a number of bad experiences from the outings it has made with its previous owner.

AGGRESSION

In the questions and comments discussed I have made no reference to observable signs of aggression. These should not be displayed by a well-balanced puppy. If on any occasion your puppy should snap at you for no apparent reason, or for minimal reason, such as when you go to pick it up or to touch a given part of

To combat boredom and relieve your puppy's natural desire to chew, there's nothing better than a Roar-Hide™. Unlike common rawhide, this bone won't turn into a gooey mess when chewed on, so your dog won't choke on small pieces of it, and your carpet won't be stained by it. The Roar-Hide™ is completely edible and is high in protein (over 86%) and low in fat (less than 1/3 of 1%). The regular-sized Roar-Hide™ is just right for your puppy. Available at your local pet shop.

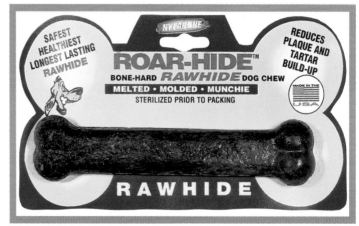

its body, then the puppy has a problem. There are basically two types of aggression, one is seen within the dominant type dog that wishes to be a pack leader, the other is fear aggression where the puppy will bite or make threats because it feels threatened itself. Both types have the potential to be dangerous, the dominant type being the more so. However, the dog that has fear aggression can be unpredictable, and is the sort that will snap at people if it thinks they are not looking. Aggression in puppies is often brought about by their being teased in any of many ways. It may also have been induced by a puppy being disturbed persistently when it is asleep, by being played with too roughly, or because it has copied the actions of its mother and siblings in its previous home.

UTILIZING YOUR OBSERVATIONS

Once you have made a preliminary observation of your puppy in a number of situations you can then determine the needed course of action. Most often, where there is the likelihood of previous mistreatment, or a lack of treatment, the answer is to take the complete opposite course. For example, if your puppy shows fear, or at the least apprehension,

A puppy that is fearful will approach new objects, people and situations with caution. He may also be prone to unpredictable displays of aggression if he feels threatened.

of strangers, it is important that it be introduced to as many people as possible, and as soon as possible. Such introduction should of course always result in the stranger speaking softly to the puppy and lavishing praise on it. If a puppy

Every puppy likes to wrestle and roughhouse, but displays of aggression or dominant tendencies in your puppy can indicate a real problem that might become dangerous if not curbed immediately.

shows undue interest in trash cans, these should be removed so the pup cannot get at them. If it shows concern at being touched on certain parts of its body you should endeavor to touch these often—but never by forcibly restraining the puppy. Do this when it is tired, and in a gentle manner.

SCORING OBSERVATIONS

If you wish to score your puppy's reactions to given situations you should select those actions that are clearly negatives or undesirables ahead of those which are normal. The latter will be given a score of zero. You could then grade on a 1-5 basis for behavior patterns that need alteration, 5 being the most undesirable state. Your objective is thus to reach that point when the puppy will have a nil score.

However, you must make every effort to be very consistent in the way you apply marks to your observations, otherwise the end picture will be distorted. Done correctly, and by continually striving to arrest problems and move behavior in the desired direction, you should see a steady improvement in behavior. This will allow the true genetic personality of your puppy to be revealed. If your puppy is of the timid type, nothing will ever make it a bold, outgoing

If your pup seems timid or reserved around people, treat him gently and introduce him to strangers who will praise and encourage him.

puppy. If it is the latter, only careful restraint will prevent it from becoming the pack leader in your home, and thus a potentially very dangerous dog when it matures, the more so if it is a medium to large dog.

Although the comments I have made with regards to observations may seem as though I am indicating the puppy's personality, this is not the case. The comments are generalizations for you to use as the basis for your continued observations.

They provide a guide to what is a normal reaction. An abnormal reaction is more indicative of how the puppy has been previously treated than an indicator of its true character. You are not making categoric assertions based on these, because they will be changing from day to day, especially over the first few weeks. You can only unlock the true personality of your puppy over months of working with it on a regular basis. There really are no shortcuts to this reality.

Knowing your puppy's personality will assist you in training him to become a valued family member and a true friend.

CHINESE SHAR-PEI

How Does Your Puppy Learn?

If you are unaware of how your puppy learns you will have far more problems training it and will be at a loss to understand why things go wrong and how to correct them. You will be more likely to indiscriminately punish your puppy—and at inappropriate moments.

Leads are available to prevent dogs of any size or weight from pulling under any circumstances. Photo courtesy of Four Paws.

This Cocker Spaniel puppy will not understand the words you say to him, he will only associate certain actions with the volume and tone of your voice.

This will badly affect its ability to be correctly trained.

MISCONCEPTIONS & TRUTHS

Before we discuss the learning process let us get a few misconceptions out of the way first.

1. Your puppy does not reason things out, it does not moralize on its actions, and it does not have pride in what it does. It does not understand your words, it can only associate given actions or your desires with certain sounds that are vocalized by you in different volume, length, and pitch.

2. Your puppy has no sense of good or bad in a human context, only what gives it enjoyment and what does not, what is acceptable and what is not. An adult dog would be quite happy to kill your pet rabbit and eat it. This would be a wholly natural thing for it to do. That it will not is because you train it not to.

3. Never attribute human qualities to your dog. Of course, you will do this when talking to friends about your dog, or

Car safety is something you have to assist your puppy with. This pet safety sitter is designed to secure your pup or dog in place in the car, keeping him from disturbing the driver and other passengers. Courtesy of Four Paws.

to your dog, but never take such comments seriously as many owners clearly do, otherwise you will begin to believe they are real. The most important trait of your puppy, and one you should always be aware of, is that it lives for the moment, not for the past or the future. Your puppy can never be guilty of deceit, dishonesty, or shame, but it can exhibit jealousy and cunning. It can harbor resentment, and does not display compassion. It will display trust and loyalty to a degree not seen in any other animal, and the latter can include humans. It can exhibit an excellent

memory, and may display great patience. But it is a dog, not a human.

THE POWER OF REASONING

Intelligence in any creature, including humans, is a combination of memory, instinct, and reason. The latter is highly dependent on the amount of memory that the individual has. To what degree any of the mammals other than the primates (monkeys, apes, and humans) are able to reason things out is very debatable. For all practical purposes you should not presume your dog can reason. If you do, you will create more problems for yourself in how you relate to the dog than if you assume it has no such powers. When dogs and

It is very important to remember that your puppy has no concept of past or future, but only lives for the moment. Therefore, he is incapable of feeling human emotions like regret or shame when he misbehaves.

other mammals apparently display the power to reason, this is invariably because the owner has misinterpreted what they believe has happened. Trainers of birds, horses, dogs, and other animals are able to teach their animals to do things that appear to be the result of reasoning, but it is an illusion, just like the feats of those who are gifted at tricks of apparent magic.

INSTINCT

An instinct is doing what comes naturally to a given creature. It is a trait best viewed as a natural evolutionary response to any given situation. Animal behaviorists call it phyletic memory. An example would be for an animal to move away from a source of pain—such as a fire—without even thinking about the matter. All animals, including humans, rely a lot on phyletic memory to determine the course of action that is most conducive to ensuring they stay alive. This may be with respect to eating, including the procurement of foods, moving away from obvious dangers, defending oneself, or simply moving from one area to another in order to be remain within a favorable environment.

Your puppy instinctively urinates and defecates whenever or wherever it wants to. It will instinctively seek out food even though it may not be especially hungry at that particular moment, and it will instinctively seek the most comfortable place in which to rest or sleep. It will likewise instinctively

When training your puppy, you must remember that there is no such thing as a "bad" dog! Dogs do not understand that their behavior can have negative consequences.

chase rabbits, sheep, or anything else that in the wild might represent its next meal. The same natural drives mean that it will defend its home and pack members, and it will howl when it is lonely and wants to communicate with others. It will bark when it senses potential intruders to its domain.

If you think carefully about all of these quite natural actions you will find that they are the very ones that pose the greatest problems to us dog owners. It is thus not easy for your puppy to make the transition from wild to living in a domesticated state with humans. Most of its instincts are regarded as undesirable to us if they are uncontrolled. The point here is that what you perceive of as being bad in a dog or puppy is not really so; rather, it is undesirable if uncontrollable.

The proper balance of nutrients builds a healthy mind as well as body. Helps protect against dietary allergies while promoting healthy skin and coat. Photo courtesy of Nature's Recipe Pet Foods.

Unfortunately, some owners seem to think that their dogs should automatically know what they should and should not do.

Training your puppy is thus all about modifying basic instincts so that they are not offensive to you. Do this and you have a nice puppy; fail and you have a delinquent dog that will rely on its instincts to determine any course of action. Viewed in this context you will fully appreciate why there can never be a bad dog in the fullness of its meaning, only a bad dog in the way the society it lives in perceives good or bad. A human can be bad because a man or woman may consciously do things they know to be alien to our way of life. Your dog can never be guilty of this sort of bad because it is not one of our species and does not think like us or perceive life as we do. That's why it is a dog and not a human—a point a lot of owners seem to forget!

MEMORY

With reason and instincts placed into perspective we come to the last component of intelligence, which is memory. This and this alone is the basis of how your puppy will learn to modify its instincts. It will not sit and think about reasons why it should and should not do this or that, but it will simply scan its memory to tell it how it should react. The better its powers of memory recall, the quicker and the more it will learn. The greater the range of memories it has, the more predictable it will be. In other words it will display what we perceive to be, and call, sound temperament.

Your puppy's memory can be regarded as a storage box for one of three sorts of stimuli. These are positive, passive, or negative. A positive memory is one of pleasure or success; a negative is one which was painful or failed to achieve an objective; a passive stimuli is neither of the other two. What you should understand is that a memory can range from positive through passive to negative and vice versa. Ideally, you want your puppy's to contain these three basic components in a very consistent form so it will never be confused or stressed as a result of having mixed-up memories.

If you gave your puppy a big hug and lots of kisses when it came to meet you

Every animal has natural instincts that help him survive in the wild. Unfortunately, many of these instincts are the obstacles you must overcome in order to produce a well-trained dog.

at the door, this would obviously be a very positive stimuli. If you smacked it every time it came to greet you, this would be totally negative. In the former instance it would always rush to you, in the latter it would quickly learn to get as far

Your dog should associate being with you as a pleasant experience. If you yell at or scold your puppy every time he comes to you, he will end up being frightened, which defeats the whole purpose of training him yourself.

running to you is its *reaction* (and an action in itself). Your hugging the puppy is a reaction to what the puppy has done, but again an action of itself. The same applies to the sequence when it is smacked.

If these actions on your behalf are consistent, the puppy is able to make the choice of what action it wishes to take in reply to yours, and it will rely on its memory of past happenings in that situation to determine what it should do. If the puppy wishes to be hugged it will rush to you, thus the consequence of doing so will be known to the puppy in advance,

away from you as possible when you came through the door. But what if you hugged it sometimes, and other times you smacked it, based on how your day at work had been? Your puppy gets two contrasting stimuli to the same action (your coming through the door). Clearly, the puppy will not know from day to day which reaction it should display to you. The result is total confusion and frustration.

When the puppy can no longer *determine events by its own actions*, you have a problem puppy. Understanding this is the very heart and soul of successful training. When you enter the door, that is an *action*. Your puppy

Your puppy needs to understand that for every action he commits, you will respond with a reaction that is either positive or negative. When he knows that a certain action will provoke a negative reaction from you, he is less likely to do something that is forbidden—like rooting through the garbage!

thus the puppy controls the result of its own actions. The same theory applies to everything else your puppy does. If the consequence of a given action results in a negative stimuli, every time, it will drop that particular behavior pattern in favor of an alternative action that would have resulted in either a positive or a passive consequence.

There is always an alternative choice the puppy can make. For example, the alternative to jumping up is not to jump up; to pulling when being walked on a lead is not to pull; to raiding your garbage is not to do this. But the puppy must be taught these things. It will never do them of its own choice, because the required behavior is invariably unnatural to the puppy.

In certain instances it is vital that you facilitate the alternative, otherwise the puppy obviously cannot choose. For example, the alternative to peeing on your carpet is to do it in your yard. But if you keep the puppy locked up in your home for hours at a time, then there is no choice for the puppy but to attend to its needs anywhere in your home. If an owner cannot display enough intelligence to reason this out, then they must be prepared to suffer the consequences of their own stupidity. Sadly, the

poor dog often has to pay the price of such stupidity by being disciplined or banished into the yard, thus making it fearful of its owners for something it had no control over, but which its owner most certainly did.

THE TIME FACTOR

The final factor you must understand in knowing how a puppy learns is that of time in relation to any given stimuli. Consider the following: If someone came

Puppies and dogs (and people!) are more inclined to repeat something that has a positive association—and food is definitely positive to a dog. These treats are not only tasty, but highly digestible and naturally preserved to protect against dietary sensitivities. Photo courtesy of Nature's Recipe Pet Foods.

up to you and said "No" in a firm voice, or if they actually hit you, what would you think and how would you react? You might hit them back, or at the least you would ask

why they were saying no to you. After all, you were doing nothing wrong at that time. In the absence of an explanation, you would assume that the "No" was in some way related to what you were doing at the moment the word was said. Even if you were told it was because you did something minutes or hours before, you would still have to figure out which of all your recent actions was regarded as wrong.

If you would be left feeling frustrated and confused after such a happening, what do you think this same situation would do to your puppy? Since it does not reason like you, it would simply assume the admonishment was for what it was doing at the precise moment it was told "No."

Nowhere is this time factor so misunderstood as when owners call their puppies to them and then discipline them for something undesirable. An obvious example: The puppy messed on the carpet so it is called and then taken by the scruff of the neck, shown the little pile of fecal matter, and either shouted at or smacked. The puppy records two simple memories. One, the owner called and it responded. Two, the owner then manhandled it, shouted at it, or spanked it. That and that alone is what will go into its memory. In other words, it will relate responding to its name with being yelled at or spanked.

However, at other times that same action—going to the owner—will result in petting and praise. Can you see what is happening? Positive and negative consequences to the same action. How many times have you seen a dog that, when called, goes to its owner in a cowed manner, crawling as it got near to them, rolling over, or even urinating, yet wagging its tail at the same time? Such a sight is always sad to see because it tells you what the owner never would. The poor dog does not know what to expect when it gets to them, yet it wants to be near them. It has clearly been spanked a number of times when it reached the owner. Dogs never lie, they cannot speak, but they can tell all by their actions of how they are treated by their owner.

Let us return to the example given, messing on the carpet. The owner is crediting the dog with the ability to reason that it is being punished not for going to the owner, but for messing on the carpet. The owner thinks that by showing the dog the mess this should register the point. But it does not. You could show that little pile or puddle to Fido all day long and that's all it would be to it, a pile of excrement. If it has messed on the carpet it is because it had not been taught what the alternative was. Further, even it did understand what it should do, this presupposes it had the opportunity to do this when that need arose, which clearly could not have been the case. So, when training your puppy or dog, all stimuli, be they positive or negative, must be registered in the puppy's memory to coincide with the action you wish to reinforce or to change. The puppy cannot relate backwards by what you tell it, but it will relate backwards to its memory to determine

Try to catch your dog in the act of misbehaving before correcting him, otherwise he will not understand the reason for his punishment. Encourage good behavior by offering him safe fun toys like Nylafloss®.

Encourage your puppy's good behavior with a special treat, like a Gumabone® Wishbone®. They are made of non-toxic, durable polyurethane, and have a texture that your puppy will enjoy sinking his teeth into—and the chewed ends develop frays that act as a toothbrush to break up plaque. Available at your local pet shop.

an action at any given moment. If there is no memory to draw on, it will rely on its instincts. Always remember that if you punish your puppy in the present for something done in the past, it will relate what is happening at that moment to the punishment, and this invariably means coming to you when called!

Again, how many times have you seen a dog move away with its head lowered and tail between its legs when the owner says, "Who's done this?" in response to messing, or tearing up something, or raiding the trash can. What often follows is, "See, he knows he's been a naughty boy!" The owner

One action you can be sure your puppy will repeat is his trip to the food bowl. Fill it with a 100% complete and balanced food that does not contain wheat, corn or soy, and so is excellent for dogs with dietary sensitivities. Photo courtesy of Nature's Recipe Pet Foods.

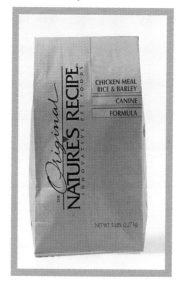

has missed the point entirely. The dog clearly understands the tone the phrase is said in and associates this with the wallopings it has had in the past. Of course it clears off, tail between legs. It doesn't know what it has done wrong at all, it just doesn't want another good hiding for no reason it can relate to!

You must constantly remind yourself, until it is ingrained in your mind, that your puppy or dog should never be disciplined for an act unless it is at the very moment of doing it. Try to relate to the wild dog. In its life there is never any question of punishment for a past happening, only for one in the present. The outcome of this, be it a bite from another wolf or being charged by a moose, is recorded in the young wolf's mind and can be related to the next time that same situation arises. This is how it learns by its own successes and mistakes.

To your puppy, life is a long series of happenings that either have good, bad, or neutral conclusions. These all get filed in its memory so they can be referred to the next time they happen. But you or I are really no different. How many times have you done something only to vow it's the last because the outcome was hardly beneficial to your general welfare. You learn by your mistakes. Sometimes such mistakes lose you time, or cost you money. Others may result in a painful conclusion. In spite of the latter you may make the same mistake again until the lesson is well learned.

Above: Housebreaking is an integral part of preparing your puppy to live in your home as part of your family. Left: Knowing your puppy's personality and the way he thinks gives you the advantage in training him and makes it easier to acclimate him to the rules of your home. Below: Your dog remembers if certain situations resulted in a positive, negative, or neutral ending. He will refer to these memories before doing something in order to predict the outcome of his actions.

PIT BULL TERRIER

Housebreaking 101

Training a puppy to be clean in its new home is a priority for every owner. This is not a difficult thing to do providing you understand a few simple facts about the entire process of defecation in relation to canines. There are two ways in which a puppy can be taught to

Paper training is one way to approach toilet training your puppy, or, if you have one of the very small breeds, a litter box can also be used.

attend to its toilet needs. One is by housebreaking, which by definition means the puppy will go outside to relieve itself. The other is paper training, whereby the puppy relieves itself on paper or, if it is a very small breed, in a litter box provided by you for this purpose.

Some trainers will state that you must choose one or other method from the

The term housebreaking means training your dog to relieve himself outside. Always keep your puppy on a leash to prevent him from becoming separated from you.

outset and stick with it because you cannot paper train a puppy on a temporary basis and then expect it to go outdoors later. The claim is that it confuses the puppy. I have no problems with your choosing one method and sticking with it. But I have to disagree with anyone who says that the puppy cannot change from paper or a litter box to going outdoors. Forty years of dog and cat ownership tell me this is just not so. Your

puppy has a tremendous ability to adjust to new situations providing he understands what is expected of him. This is why a dog with problems can be retrained in the right hands. It is also why you can commence with paper training and progress without any

Although some say that it is best to choose one housebreaking method and stick with it, dogs are very adaptable and can be retrained if necessary.

problems to housebreaking as long as you go about it in a sensible manner and reinforce the desired action when it is needed.

Before discussing the way you should toilet-train your puppy, it is actually beneficial to discuss the problems that are created when the pup is not trained carefully. This will underscore the reason why it must be confined until it is duly trained and why many owners have problems with their dogs, and even cats, that foul the home on an apparently indiscriminate basis.

The scenting power of all dogs is extremely good, and infinitely better than that of humans to certain organic compounds found in fecal matter, sweat, and similar odors. When a dog urinates, the odors do not stay in the immediate spot that was used. Using a disinfectant to clean the spot will not remove the scent for two reasons. First, disinfectants tend to

Speed up your paper training by using a housebreaking pad to attract your puppy to a particular spot. These are lined with plastic to prevent damage to floors and carpets. Courtesy of Four Paws.

Crates are great housebreaking tools because dogs do not like to soil where they sleep. They are also useful for keeping your dog safe when you are not around to supervise him.

mask rather than break down nitrogenous compounds. They lose their power as time passes by, but the molecules that make up the scent remain on the carpet. Equally important, they are applied some distance from the actual spot used, so that cleaning must encompass a much wider area than would seem to be necessary. You might not be able to detect an odor when it is masked, but your dog will have no such problem. Further, the scent will travel to mark furniture and any material that will absorb it.

Once the puppy has posted its scent, and especially if you have not noticed where this was done, it will return to this spot unless you restrict it from that spot or you thoroughly neutralize the scent. Neutralizing requires a special chemical compound; pet supply stores and veterinarians carry products with the right ingredients. When using such a compound, you should neutralize quite a wide area from the spot marked. You can see why it is preferable to not let a problem develop than to have to overcome one.

PAPER (OR LITTER BOX) TRAINING

Whether you paper or litter box train your puppy is a matter decided upon by yourself, and to some degree determined by the size of your puppy, its sex and breed. Small males, and females up to medium size, can be paper or litter box trained. Larger breeds of males will need housebreaking, as will females unless you are able to provide a very large litter box.

The basis of total paper or litter box training is that the puppy will attend to its needs on or in this throughout its life. It is a convenient method for owners living in high-rise apartments who do not have immediate access to a yard. It is far less suited to dogs than to bitches because of the former's need to raise a leg and urinate to a high point.

The way to paper train a puppy is to associate in his mind that the place to

Paper or litter box training is more suited to people that own small breeds of dogs or owners that live in urban areas or apartments and do not have easy access to the outdoors.

The key to paper training is to leave a small amount of soiled newspaper down so that your puppy can pick up this scent. Dogs tend to eliminate in the same spot, and the scent will be the marker to tell the pup where to go.

relieve himself you can go to him, lift him up gently, and take him to the desired spot. Much praise should be given if he does as expected. A puppy wanting to relieve himself will tend to move around the kitchen (or whichever area you choose), sniffing the floor and probably whimpering. He may turn in small circles as well.

Always try to preempt errors by watching the puppy at the times when he will want to relieve himself. If you have been consistent in paper training, you should find that the puppy is attending to his needs in the required area within seven to ten days of arriving in your home. It is a rather inconvenient method because it means your kitchen must have paper down throughout the period, but in the long run you will be glad you made the effort.

Litter box training is done in the same manner, but in this instance a litter box is placed in the required location, on top of the papers. Whenever the puppy is seen beginning to attend to his needs, lift him up and place him into the box. Praise profusely when he does as desired. Gradually reduce the paper covering on the floor in the same way as paper training. A small amount of fecal matter can be placed into the box to provide the needed scent

defecate is at a given spot in the home. To train the puppy, you must first cover the entire floor with a double layer of newspaper sheets so he cannot foul an inappropriate area. Praise the puppy effusively when you see him attending to his needs. Remove the soiled paper, but leave a small amount of urinated paper under a fresh sheet. The odor from this will attract the puppy to the

same spot the next time he wishes to relieve himself. Move the scented paper towards the ultimate toilet spot. At the same time, remove one or two sheets from the furthest point from where you want the puppy to go, assuming he has used the same spot over two or three days. Neutralize the spot you don't want the puppy going in.

If you are present when the puppy is about to

for the puppy. By placing the pup in the box after he has played, awoken from sleep, or eaten, he will eventually get the message and oblige you.

Once you see that the puppy is using the litter box, it is important to keep it very clean of any fecal matter or urine. The very act of using the litter box will be an internalized reinforcer, so fecal matter from the previous use does not need to remain in the box. Neither dogs nor cats like to walk into a soiled litter box. Problems can often arise because the owners do not clean them after each use. Failure to provide a suitably larger box as the puppy grows can also result in problems.

HOUSEBREAKING A PUPPY

There is no magic formula for successfully housebreaking a puppy; rather, it's a straightforward process that includes three key elements. You must be consistent, patient and reasonable. *Consistency* involves setting a schedule for yourself and your puppy from which you must never vary for at least a few weeks, and only slightly after that. You'll need *patience* because your puppy will make mistakes. Expect them and handle them correctly, and they'll soon dwindle and disappear. Last but not least, you

need to be *reasonable*—about where and when you want your puppy to eliminate, about how long the process could take, and about evaluating your own role in the training.

The first thing to do is set up a schedule. It will vary depending on the age of your puppy. Since puppies need to eliminate after meals, count on making trips to the potty spot at least three times a day. They also need to go first thing in the morning, about 20 minutes after drinking, before they go to bed at night (and for very young puppies once during the night), and when they wake up from naps. This means that you will have to escort your three- to four-month-old puppy outside every few

hours.

What you want to do is prevent the puppy from having an accident, and praise him for doing what you want. That means taking him outside at the right times and anytime you see him circling, sniffing the floor, squatting or acting as if he's about to relieve himself. At these times, pick the puppy up and take him outside to the spot you want him to use. Use a phrase like "Potty time" to let him know what you want, and when he's finished, praise him lavishly. Don't praise in the middle of the act or you could distract him from finishing.

Since you can't watch him 24 hours a day, until he's reliably housetrained you'll have to confine him

Puppies usually have to go to the bathroom just after eating, drinking, waking up or strenuous play, so do not ignore any signs your puppy may give you that he has to go out.

to a safe area. This can be a crate (which your puppy will soon come to think of as his own comfy retreat) or the kitchen. Don't isolate him. Dogs are very social animals and isolation will seem like a punishment, which could lead to more problems than cures where housebreaking's concerned.

If the puppy is taken to a predetermined area on a regular basis he will use the spot—and he'll get lavish praise from you when he does. If he needs to go to the toilet when the kitchen door is closed, he will automatically use his litter box. He should have no problem using either if he is encouraged to do so. The transition from litter box (or paper) to garden does not happen overnight, but always happens over just a few weeks. By preference, a puppy will choose a yard to a litter box or paper every time; it is a far more natural choice. After a time the puppy will cease using his box providing he is taken out on a regular basis, which all puppies should be. With each passing week, the puppy is a little more able to control his bowels.

ENSURING SUCCESS

From this discussion you should be able to train your puppy to be clean in your home. However, you must bear in mind that

certain conditions must prevail in order to ensure success:

1. The puppy must be confined to a given area, preferably one that has an easily cleaned floor, such as the kitchen. This confinement must be maintained until the puppy is paper or litter box trained or housebroken.

2. Do not make the toilet area too close to either food or water dishes. No animal likes to defecate or urinate near to its food.

3. Stick to the schedule: The puppy must be fed at

To ensure housetraining success, make sure your puppy is in good health and stick to a regular feeding schedule. This makes it easier to predict approximately when your dog will need to relieve himself.

Make sure your puppy gets plenty of exercise and ample time to play outdoors. This provides him with the opportunity to use his new skills and relieve himself outside.

regular times so you are able to more readily know when he is likely to want to relieve himself.

4. The puppy must be in good health. If he has diarrhea he will clearly be unable to control his bowels for even a few moments, and will have accidents.

5. The puppy must be exercised *at least* three times every day. This provides the needed opportunity for him to relieve himself.

6. Once the puppy is housetrained, you must respond promptly when he clearly indicates he wishes to go outside. If you ignore

his pleas because you are doing something else, you merely force the dog to relieve himself in your home.

7. Always praise success.

8. Avoid the temptation to reprimand your pet if you see him going to a spot that is other than where he should go. Simply walk up to him, lift him up and take him to the desired area. A "No" is justifiable only if the puppy is caught in the act. Then immediately take him to the desired spot, place him down and praise him after he goes where you want.

9. If you do decide to litter box train as a pre-housebreaking method, do not suddenly remove the litter box and expect the puppy not to foul the space the box or paper previously occupied. Leave the box in place until you are sure the puppy is old enough to control his bowels and is going outside every single day. This will become an internalized reinforcer and the previous habit of using the litter box will be dropped before it is a deep-seated behavior pattern.

10. Finally, remember that you may be legally responsible for gathering up any fecal matter your dog deposits when outside of your property. No one likes to walk where dogs have left a pile of fecal

Do not make your puppy's designated toilet area a place that is too close to his food or shelter.

matter. It is also essential, from a health viewpoint, to regularly remove and dispose of fecal matter from your yard and garden.

HOUSEBREAKING AN OLDER DOG

Training an older dog to eliminate outside of the house may take longer than training a puppy, but it works the same way. Confine the dog to an area that can be easily cleaned; if necessary, paper the floor and gradually remove most of the paper as discussed above. Stick to a schedule of taking the dog out a half hour or so after he eats or drinks. Praise lavishly when he goes when and where you want him to. Do not punish mistakes unless you catch the dog in the act, at which time you'll need to carry or lead him outside

to the designated spot and praise him for finishing there.

It's especially important to neutralize the odors of any mistakes an older dog makes, since old habits die harder. You may want to crate-train the older dog at

Buy a crate for your dog made of either fiberglass or wire, and make sure it is big enough for him to fit in comfortably. Make it appealing to your dog by lining it with a soft blanket and placing treats inside.

the same time that you housebreak him. Remember, you'll need lots of patience with an older dog. Hang in there, and if problems persist, consult a veterinarian or professional trainer.

CRATE TRAINING

To acclimate a dog who wasn't crate-trained as a puppy to the crate, you'll need the correct size crate and, again, patience. Buy a crate in which the adult can comfortably stand, turn around and lie down. Nothing bigger, nothing smaller. Make the crate an appealing place. Put an old, clean towel or blanket on the crate floor. At first, just leave the crate door open and let your dog explore it on his own. Toss some treats in the crate and let him retrieve them. Gradually, begin to feed the dog in the crate, starting with the bowl near the door and then moving it toward the back—always with the door open.

When the dog seems comfortable inside the crate, toss in a treat, use a command like "In the crate," close the door and walk away. Ignore the dog for a few minutes, and if he isn't whining or crying, praise him then let him out. Slowly build up the time you leave him in the crate with the door closed. If you make the crate a pleasant place and crate-training a rewarding experience, your dog will soon be seeking out his crate whenever he needs some R&R, and will be happy to be confined in it when you need him out of harm's way for a short while.

You should get your dog accustomed to his crate. This wire crate not only provides your dog with his own haven from the world, but it provides a safe way for him to travel in a car.

Your puppy's mental and emotional well-being are just as important as his physical health. Make sure he is happy and comfortable as a member of your family.

DOBERMAN PINSCHER

When Things Aren't Working

Years ago the term stress was rarely used because it was poorly understood. Certain behavioral problems were viewed as side effects of poor nutrition or even fear. But with more and more studies being done, the importance of recognizing stress as a major cause of numerous problems has steadily increased. Today it is generally agreed that stress factors are possibly the singular most important precursors of both physical and behavioral problems. A stressed animal is much more likely to become ill than one that is not.

Children can inadvertently put stress on your puppy, which can be an underlying factor if your dog is experiencing any physical or behavioral problems. Dustin and his young Yorkie friends, however, seem to be getting along just fine!

An animal that is under stress or is experiencing boredom may show signs of behavior problems. Giving your puppy a Nylabone® is an excellent way to fight boredom while strengthening his teeth and jaws.

Recovery will also be prolonged. Further, unwanted behavior problems, called syndromes, are likely to develop.

WHAT IS STRESS?

Stress may be defined as any factor within an environment that creates subconscious distress or an odd behavior pattern. Whenever an animal cannot go about a normal way of living, it will invariably become stressed, producing physical and psychological

Stress can be caused by a well-meaning child bothering or teasing your puppy. Always supervise your children when they play with your dog and never leave the child and dog unattended.

changes for the worse. One of the problems with stress is that it can be very difficult to identify in an individual because two animals may react totally differently to similar situations. Also, it could be that an improper diet (which is itself unnatural) can create stress, which in turn results in undesirable behavior patterns becoming established.

Stress is complex. It can be induced by constantly waking a puppy (children are often guilty of this); teasing a puppy; excessive noise, especially that which is high-pitched; and, naturally, the transition from the security of its mother to a new home. That's why the first couple of weeks in a new home are so important to the puppy and how it will develop as a dog.

In theory, if you remove the stress factors from the animal's environment it would seem logical to assume that unwanted behavior patterns would disappear. In reality this is not always the case. Examples of stress-induced behavior patterns are numerous, and only a few will be discussed here so you can relate to the cause, effects and treatment of the condition.

EXAMPLES OF STRESS CONDITIONS

1. Destructive Behavior. This is often the

consequence of close confinement in dogs and other animals. It may also result from frustration born out of inconsistent discipline by an owner. The immediate remedy must be to overcome the underlying cause. Next, the problems created by the cause must be addressed. Depending on how ingrained these are as patterns of behavior will depend how successful the corrections are. Removal of all reinforcers is the most obvious means of overcoming destructive behavior—coupled with consistent basic training.

2. Pacing.

This is commonly seen in confined zoo animals, but is also characteristic of both dogs and horses that are confined to small pens or pounds. The dog will create a beaten path where it paces back and forth. Sometimes the condition will show itself in head weaving when confinement is very close, such as when left in a crate excessively. An immediate remedy is to give the dog more space and more exercise.

3. Self Mutilation and Excessive Licking.

Both of these syndromes (including tail biting) are the consequence of excessive confinement and the frustration that comes with it. Here confinement can expand to include boredom through loneliness. These syndromes can also result

Dogs that are confined to small spaces for long periods of time can experience stress-induced behavior problems, like pacing. Allow your puppy plenty of room to exercise and as much space as possible.

Some behavior problems may be due to a lack of nutrients or a less-than-adequate diet. Always make sure your puppy is getting well-balanced meals designed to suit his nutritional needs.

from abusive punishment and/or acute nervousness. When your puppy is left alone, it should always have something to play with to occupy its mind.

However, both self mutilation and licking can indicate a medical problem. Check with your veterinarian when the unwanted behavior has a physical manifestation.

4. Sucking in Puppies.

This is commonly seen in puppies that are weaned too early. The behavior develops as the puppy looks for a

Puppies, like this eight-week-old Chesapeake Bay Retriever, love to chew on things. If you give him constructive chew toys, like Nylabones®, he will be more likely to stay away from things he finds in the wilderness that may be potentially harmful.

substitute for its mother and sucks on various items including its paws. The condition generally ceases as the pup matures if it is in a happy home. If not, the behavior could continue and become worse. Such a puppy needs special attention even before training begins.

5. Coprophagia (Eating Feces).

This is clearly a repugnant habit for a dog living with humans. There

Puppies love to play, no matter how small they are, so keep your puppy busy with lots of fun activities. This Yorkie wants to play ball, even if the ball is as big as him!

are numerous causes, not all of which are stress related. Pups in the three- to nine-month-old range may eat feces, but this usually ceases upon maturity. What causes pups to continue the behavior?

The problem could be inadequate nutrients in the diet or gastrointestinal upset. It could be caused

Offer your puppy praise and a treat — like this Nylabone® Wishbone®—if he does what is expected of him.

by living in dirty or overcrowded conditions; acute nervousness; or the practice by some owners of rubbing the puppy's nose in a mistake. In the latter, the pup may lick its nose and find something satisfying in the fecal matter, thus reinforcing the behavior.

Assuming the problem is not nutritionally based, the ways to overcome or avoid it are various. The best is to maintain scrupulous hygiene by removing fecal matter immediately and disposing of it properly. If you can monitor the pup's toilet habits stringently, correcting it when it tries to eat the feces you're

These lucky Bichon pups have a variety of Nylabone® toys to play with. Safe chew toys keep puppy teeth occupied and out of trouble.

Why would you want to give your dog a Carrot Bone™? Because you know carrots are rich in fiber, carbohydrates and vitamin A. Because it's a durable chew containing no plastics or artificial ingredients of any kind. Because it can be served as-is, in bone-hard form, or microwaved to a biscuity consistency — whichever your dog prefers. Because its a 100%-natural plaque, obesity and boredom fighter for your dog. Available at your local pet shop.

removing, you can effectively eliminate the problem.

TRAINING SUMMARY

Remember, it is infinitely easier to avoid problems than to have to correct them. Start by establishing a strong bond of affection with the puppy, then start to apply discipline gently but firmly. Always lavish praise for success and be consistent with all of your actions, be these for success or for discipline. Always try to think why the puppy does what it does—have you unwittingly encouraged a behavior you now find undesirable? If a corrective action is needed, can this be achieved by praising an alternative pattern of behavior or by removing the cause? This is always preferable to discipline.

When discipline is needed, do not shirk your

Your puppy needs to learn basic commands, not only for your benefit, but for his safety.

Your mannerly dog, like this Golden Retriever, will get along with anyone or anything!

responsibility in effecting it. In the long run it is in the best interests of the

Keep your puppy continually challenged by teaching him new tricks and providing him with plenty of opportunity to exercise. These smiling Rottie pups look like they are having a great time exploring the yard.

puppy. Never allow your feelings of the moment to override sensible and fair judgment. Always remember that your puppy lives in the present, never in the future or past.

Do not try to achieve too much too soon, but build day by day based on success rather than concentrating too much on failures. Once the puppy has become an integral part of your family and life, do not let it become bored. Practice what it already knows, but do so in a pleasurable rather than drill-sergeant

fashion. Try to think of games and tricks you can teach your puppy every week so it is continually being challenged. And don't skimp on exercise, including walks on leash.

Never forget that your puppy is born neither good nor bad, just a puppy. What it becomes will be determined by the way you rear and train it. Its main desire in life is to be happy and do whatever it takes to ensure that state prevails. With your guidance, both of you will enjoy many years of loving companionship.

An untrained and ill-mannered dog is not only a nuisance, but can be a danger to others.

Suggested Reading

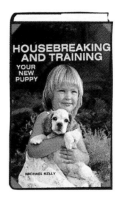

**Training The Perfect
Puppy**
By Andrew De Prisco
JG-109
160 pages, over 200 color photos.

Successful Dog Training
By Michael Kramer, OSB
TS-205
160 pages, over 150 color photos.

**Housebreaking Your
New Puppy**
By Michael Kelly
TU-011
64 pages, full color photos.

**Housebreaking Your
Puppy, Step By Step**
By Jack C. Harris
SK-025
64 pages, over 50 color photos.

Basic Dog Training
By Miller Watson
KW-022
96 pages, over 100 color photos.

**Everybody Can Train
Their Own Dog**
By Angela White
TW-113
256 pages, 200 color photos.